Houston

Houston

A Downtown America Book

Charles Peifer, Jr.

Dillon Press, Inc. Minneapolis, MN 55415

Library of Congress Cataloging-in-Publication Data

Peifer, Charles.

Houston / by Charles Peifer, Jr.

(A Downtown America book)

Includes index.

Summary: Describes the past and present, neighborhoods, attractions, and festivals of Houston.

1. Houston (Tex.)—Juvenile literature. [1. Houston (Tex.)]
I. Title. II. Series.

F394.H857P45 1988   976.4'1411   88-20197

ISBN 0-87518-387-5

Dillon Press, Inc., 242 Portland Avenue South
Minneapolis, Minnesota 55415

Printed in the United States of America
1 2 3 4 5 6 7 8 9 10 97 96 95 94 93 92 91 90 89 88

To Helen, my best friend

Photographic Acknowledgments

Photographs have been reproduced through the courtesy of the Children's Museum of Houston; Steve Elmore/Tom Stack & Associates; Greater Houston Convention and Visitors Bureau; Houston Museum of Natural Science; Jim Mc-Nee/Tom Stack & Associates; Sheryl S. Mc-Nee/Tom Stack & Associates; Carl Miller; Port of Houston Authority; and Karin Snelson.

Contents

Fast Facts about Houston

Houston: Space City, City of the Future

Location: Southeast Texas, 50 miles (80 kilometers) inland from the Gulf of Mexico

Area: City, 580 square miles (1,501 square kilometers); consolidated metropolitan area, 7,422 square miles (19,223 square kilometers)

Population (1986 estimate*): City, 1,728,910; consolidated metropolitan area, 3,634,300

Major Population Groups: Whites, blacks, Hispanics

Altitude: 49 feet (14.9 meters) above sea level

Climate: Average temperature is 55°F (13°C) in January, 83°F (28°C) in July; average annual precipitation, including rain and snow, is 45 inches (114 centimeters)

Founding Date: 1836, incorporated as a city in 1839

City Flag: A white star with the city seal on a blue flag stands for the Lone Star State, Texas.

City Seal: A locomotive that stands for progress and a plow that represents agriculture mark Houston's city seal.

Form of Government: Houston's mayor, controller, and fourteen council members serve as the legislative body for two-year terms. A county judge and four commissioners serve Harris County for four-year terms.

Important Industries: Energy, marketing, banking, manufacturing, health care, space technology, tourism

*U.S. Bureau of the Census 1988 population estimates available in fall 1989; official 1990 census figures available in 1991-92.

Festivals and Parades:

January: Houston-Tenneco Marathon

February: Houston Livestock Show and Rodeo

March: Azalea Trail; Saint Patrick's Day Parade

March/April: Houston International Festival

April: Houston International Film Festival; Westheimer Colony Art Festival

May: Pin Oak Charity Horse Show; Spring Opera Festival; Cinco de Mayo celebrations

June: Juneteenth Blues Festival

July: Independence Day celebrations; Symphony Summer Festival

August: City of Houston Anniversary; Shakespeare Festival

September: Fiestas Patrias (a parade, formal ball, and other celebrations of Houston's Hispanic citizens); Annual Houston Jazz Festival

October: Greek Festival; Texas Renaissance Festival; German Oktoberfest

November: Thanksgiving Day Parade

December: Christmas and Hanukkah celebrations

For further information about festivals and parades, see agencies listed on page 56.

United States

CANADA

WASHINGTON
- Seattle
- Olympia
- Portland
- ★ Salem

OREGON

MONTANA
- ★ Helena

IDAHO
- ★ Boise

NORTH DAKOTA
- ★ Bismarck

SOUTH DAKOTA
- ★ Pierre

MINNESOTA
- Minneapolis
- ★ St. Paul

WISCONSIN
- ★ Madison
- Milwaukee

Lake Superior

Lake Huron

Lake Michigan

MICHIGAN
- Lansing ★
- Detroit

NEW HAMPSHIRE

VERMONT
- ★ Montpelier
- ★ Concord

MAINE
- ★ Augusta

MASSACHUSETTS

Lake Ontario

NEW YORK
- Albany ★
- Boston
- ★ Providence
- ★ Hartford

RHODE ISLAND

CONNECTICUT

Lake Erie

WYOMING
- Cheyenne ★

Great Salt Lake

Salt Lake City ★

NEVADA

UTAH

★ Carson City

- Sacramento ★
- San Francisco ●

CALIFORNIA

NEBRASKA

- Denver ★

COLORADO

IOWA
- Des Moines ★

- Omaha ●
- Lincoln ★

ILLINOIS
- Chicago ●
- Springfield ★

INDIANA
- Indianapolis ★

OHIO
- Cleveland ●
- Columbus ★
- Cincinnati ●

PENNSYLVANIA
- Pittsburgh ●
- Harrisburg ★

Trenton ★ New York City

- Philadelphia
- Dover ★

NEW JERSEY

DELAWARE

- Baltimore ●
- Annapolis ★
- Washington, D.C. ✪

MARYLAND

WEST VIRGINIA
- Charleston ★

- Richmond ★

VIRGINIA

- Las Vegas ●

ARIZONA
- Phoenix ★
- Tucson ●

KANSAS
- Topeka ★

- Kansas City ●
- Jefferson City ★
- St. Louis ●

MISSOURI

KENTUCKY
- Louisville ●
- Frankfort ★

- Raleigh ★

NORTH CAROLINA
- Charlotte ●

- Nashville ★

TENNESSEE

- Los Angeles ●
- San Diego ●

- Albuquerque ●
- Santa Fe ★

NEW MEXICO

- El Paso ●

- Oklahoma City ★

OKLAHOMA
- Tulsa ●

- Memphis ●

ARKANSAS
- Little Rock ★

- Columbia ●

SOUTH CAROLINA

- Atlanta ★

- Birmingham ●

ALABAMA
- Montgomery ★

GEORGIA

- Jacksonville ●

Pacific Ocean

MEXICO

Rio Grande

TEXAS

- Fort Worth ● Dallas
- San Antonio ●
- Austin ★
- Houston

LOUISIANA
- Jackson ★
- Baton Rouge ●
- New Orleans ●

MISSISSIPPI

- Tallahassee ★

FLORIDA
- St. Petersburg ●
- Tampa ●
- Miami ●

Atlantic Ocean

Gulf of Mexico

Mississippi

U.S.S.R.

ALASKA
- Anchorage ●
- Juneau ●

CANADA

- Honolulu ●

HAWAII

Houston

N

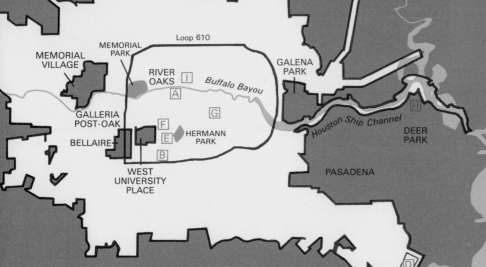

Lake Houston

Ⓒ

Loop 610

MEMORIAL
VILLAGE

MEMORIAL
PARK

RIVER
OAKS

Ⓘ *Buffalo Bayou*

Ⓐ

GALENA
PARK

GALLERIA
POST-OAK

Ⓖ

Ⓗ

BELLAIRE

Ⓕ

Ⓔ HERMANN
PARK

Houston Ship Channel

DEER
PARK

Ⓑ

WEST
UNIVERSITY
PLACE

PASADENA

Ⓓ

Galveston Bay

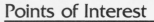

0		5		10		15		miles

0	5	10	15	20	25	30	kilometers

1

From Sea to Sky to Outer Space

Downtown Houston towers over the flatlands of southeast Texas like a chiseled mountain of glass, steel, and bricks. Jets fly overhead as cars and trucks speed along the highways that loop around the city. Houston, home to 1.7 million people, offers exciting big-city life on a grand scale.

The city stretches out on flat land in all directions, and no mountains or large bodies of water stand in its way.

A stream called the Buffalo Bayou winds through Houston and flows past the northern end of the city into the Houston Ship Channel. This important waterway leads to the Port of Houston—the third largest port in America—which connects the city to Galveston Bay, the Gulf of Mexico, and the shipping lines of the world.

In 1836, two New York real estate promoters, John and Augustus

Downtown Houston's sparkling skyscrapers loom over the horizon.

Tugboats moor along the Houston Ship Channel.

Allen, paddled up the Buffalo Bayou, fifty miles (eighty kilometers) inland from the Gulf of Mexico. The Allen brothers had big plans for the swampy land and the mosquito-infested bayou.

They bought 6,642 acres (2,690 hectares) of land near the bayou and soon began to advertise their so-called city back in the United States. (Texas wouldn't become a state until 1845.) The Allen brothers wanted people to come to the area, and hoped to make the town into the capital of the Republic of Texas.

From the start, the name of the town was its best advertisement. The brothers named the area after Sam Houston, the general who had led the army of the Republic of Texas against

The statue of Sam Houston in Hermann Park.

Santa Anna's Mexican army. On April 21, 1836, Sam Houston's army defeated the Mexican army at the battle of San Jacinto. As a result, Texas gained independence from Mexican rule. Because General Houston was now a hero, the Allen brothers felt that his name would attract people and promote their real estate venture.

It worked. With a popular name and a little "false advertising," the Allen brothers succeeded in bringing people to the area. Houston was even made the capital of the Republic of Texas from 1837 to 1839.

The development of the ship channel and the port caused Houston to grow slowly. But in 1901, the discovery of oil in east Texas changed the city forever. People poured into the city for their share in the "black gold."

Today, many large oil companies are based in Houston, and the city has been called the "energy capital of the world." Because of Houston's booming oil industry, the city was one of the first to be hit by the plunge in oil prices in the 1980s. The city has since had to develop other plans to strengthen its economy.

Houston has also become well known in other areas. Southeast of the city is the Lyndon B. Johnson Space Center. The center is the National Aeronautics and Space Administration (NASA) headquarters for astronaut training, spacecraft construction, and mission control for space flights.

The Rocket Park at NASA.

Houston's advances in medical research are known all over the world. The Texas Medical Center pioneered efforts in the treatment of cancer and heart disease. It leads the world in the numbers of heart transplants that the doctors perform—the center treats more than two million patients a year.

Over the years, Houston's growing industries have caused the city to expand to an enormous size. New buildings and an ever-growing skyline are common sights to Houstonians. The city actually has more than one

skyline—there are clusters of high-rises at several locations within the city limits.

To the southwest of downtown, the Galleria-Post Oak area's office buildings and skyscrapers could easily be mistaken for a separate city skyline.

Houston's huge downtown skyline catches the most attention. The RepublicBank Center and Pennzoil Place are famous for their architectural designs. The Texas Commerce Tower, Houston's tallest building, soars seventy-five stories into the sky.

In the middle of town, people rush around the modern art that seems to sprout like trees from concrete sidewalks. Sculptures with names such as *Personage and Birds*,

Galleria-Post Oak's sixty-four-story Transco Tower is one of the tallest buildings in the country outside of a downtown area.

This large-scale sculpture, Jean Miro's *Personage and Birds*, brightens a downtown plaza.

The Family of Man, Frozen Laces-One, and *Geometric Mouse* X are colorful and exciting works. Houston shows its interest in the arts in other ways— the Houston Grand Opera, the Houston Symphony, and the Houston Ballet all help make the city a performing arts center.

Although much of downtown Houston is made up of concrete, steel, and glass, Tranquility Park gives busy people a peaceful place to rest in the downtown area. The park is named for the Sea of Tranquility base of the Apollo 11 crew, who, in 1969, became the first humans to land on the moon. The park's green grass and sparkling fountain lure downtown workers from their offices at lunchtime. Yet even the cooling spray of water doesn't offer much relief in the summer heat.

Houston is sometimes called the most air-conditioned city in the United States. For at least six months of the year, the weather is hot and damp. The city's long heat spells feel even hotter because of the humid climate, and most Houstonians avoid spending much time outdoors under the steamy summer sun.

Even the designers of the downtown area have planned ways for people to avoid the sidewalks' baking heat. Glass-enclosed, air-conditioned skywalks span the hot streets, linking many of the buildings. Underneath the ground lies a complete system of air-conditioned walkways that are lined with shops and restaurants.

Monument au Fantome, on the corner of Louisiana and Lamar streets, was created by the French artist Jean Dubuffet.

During the winter, which lasts only about two months, it rains but rarely snows. Even in wintertime, the city has periods of warm weather—it's not uncommon to see people barbecuing in their backyards on Christmas day.

Despite its hot, humid weather, Houston has become one of America's fastest growing cities. During the 1970s and 1980s, many thousands of Americans moved here from other parts of the country to fill the many new jobs. People from Europe, South America, the Far East, and the Middle East are still streaming into Houston to work or visit.

Houston has been called the "City of the Future." As the city looks ahead, it has to deal with the problems that come with quick growth. The city's economic difficulties, crime, pollution, public transportation, and the growing numbers of homeless people continue to trouble the city. But Houston is working on ways to deal with its present problems, and to plan for the future.

Tranquility Park is often the site for outdoor summer festivities and parts of the Houston International Festival.

2

Born on the Bayou

An American Indian legend says that before the white man came, native Americans and buffalo roamed what is now Houston. There, they drank from the stream. A snow white bull led the buffalo herd, but the tribe thought it was sacred, and killed only the other buffalo for food.

One day, a white hunter killed the sacred white bull and stripped off its hide. Afraid they would be blamed for the crime, the American Indians prayed to the Great Spirit and cried for mercy for many nights.

A beautiful white-flowered magnolia tree appeared one morning on the bank of the bayou, and comforted the people. They named the stream the Buffalo Bayou and for many years called the magnolia the Buffalo Tree.

The true origin of the Buffalo Bayou's name is unknown. Yet, Houston's

The muddy Buffalo Bayou winds along Allen Parkway toward downtown Houston.

beginnings were on the bayou, and for more than a hundred years, the city has spread out and grown from that stream.

Today, it is difficult to find traces of the city's history. One sign of Houston's frontier days is downtown's Old Market Square. Alabama Coushatta Indians once galloped through the square, and wagon trains unloaded goods at the trading post. Now, a few fine restaurants occupy the otherwise empty town square.

Tucked away in a grassy area near downtown Houston is Sam Houston Park. Here, a collection of nineteenth-century buildings, including five houses, a small church, and a gazebo, stand out against the towering downtown skyscrapers.

Left: Old Saint John Church in Sam Houston Park, completed in 1891. *Right:* The mid-Victorian-style Pillot House, built in 1868, attracts visitors to Sam Houston Park.

This playground in Allen Parkway on the bayou has a good view of downtown Houston.

Just west of Sam Houston Park is Allen Parkway—a hilly, grassy park area which runs along the Buffalo Bayou. Joggers and bicyclists enjoy the landscaping and trails, and children play in the parkway's playgrounds.

The whole Buffalo Bayou area is surrounded by highway 610, or the Loop, which forms a circle around the central city. The residents who live inside the loop are sometimes called "Loopies."

In the inner loop area of River Oaks, Houston's most expensive homes and mansions are nestled along quiet, tree-lined lanes. One of these mansions, full of rare early American antiques and works of art, is called Bayou Bend. The estate was

The Bayou Bend mansion in River Oaks.

donated to Houston's Museum of Fine Arts by the late Ima Hogg. She was a member of an important family in Houston's history, and helped develop many of the city's arts organizations.

North of downtown is one of Houston's oldest neighborhoods—the Heights. Today, two- and three-story Victorian-style homes still line the streets of the Heights, and several of them are open for tours. Once a separate city, the neighborhood is now part of the city of Houston.

Many communities have become separate cities within the boundaries of Houston—and for good reason. In Houston, no zoning laws control what can be built where. As a result, neighborhoods stand next door to industries, office buildings, and even skyscrapers. These communities have their own mayors, councils, and public services such as fire and police departments.

The largest example of such a community is Bellaire, just southwest of downtown. Bellaire, which calls itself the "city of homes," tries to keep a small-town feeling within the big city that surrounds it.

In nearby Memorial Park, a jogging trail threads around the thickly wooded area, part of which is an arboretum (an area of land set aside for people to study different kinds of trees) and a nature center. The park also has a tennis center, a golf course, an archery range, and many softball diamonds.

Another such area is West University Place, which is west of Rice University, near the Texas Medical Center and the beautiful grounds of Hermann Park. Young professional people are attracted to this older, residential neighborhood by the quiet lanes, stately old trees, and exciting places to explore. In nearby Rice Village and the Montrose area, interesting shops and restaurants line the streets.

Northwest of West University Place are a cluster of small communities near the Buffalo Bayou. Hunter's Creek Village, Piney Point Village, Bunker Hill, Hilshire Village, Hedwig Village, and Spring Valley all make up Memorial Village. Here, fine neighborhoods with elegant homes are set

Memorial Park offers many recreational areas to nature-seeking Houstonians.

back in the woods, and hike-and-bike trails wind along the sides of the streets.

Southwest Houston has grown rapidly in the past ten years. Large numbers of people from the city's Oriental community live in southwest Houston. Many immigrants from the Far East have started their own businesses to serve the Vietnamese, Korean, Chinese, and Japanese communities. Often, Asian grocery stores, restaurants, and doctor's offices are grouped together in shopping plazas.

Although Asian communities are scattered throughout the city, the area known as Houston's Chinatown is very close to downtown Houston. Despite its name, most of the stores and restaurants here are Vietnamese.

Directly north and northwest of downtown are neighborhoods called wards. Here, families live in small, run-down houses and old apartment projects. But the nearness of the wards to downtown has caught the interest of developers.

Neighborhoods and communities stretch for miles outside Houston's city limits. In north Houston, neighborhoods have developed around Houston's Intercontinental Airport and Lake Houston. Huge "master-planned" communities such as the Woodlands have homes, schools, and businesses all located in one area.

To the east and southeast are the Port of Houston, oil refineries, and NASA's Johnson Space Center. These areas and industries attract

workers to suburban communities such as Galena Park, Deer Park, and Pasadena.

The city of Houston spreads out for miles and miles. Within its boundaries lie a wealth of cultures and communities. From River Oaks's mansions to Houston's wards, from the space center to the oil refineries, most newcomers seem to find their place in this fast-paced city.

3

From Dawn to Dusk

A working day in Houston starts before the sun rises. By 6:00 A.M., the main highways are jammed with cars, trucks, and buses, all moving along slowly. Drivers stuck in traffic jams tune their radios to traffic reports. Buses enter special transit lanes while the passengers' snoozing heads bob to the bumps.

An hour later, children get ready for school. Big, lumbering school buses are already on their way to pick them up. Houston's day is just beginning.

As the traffic heads toward the downtown area, it seems as if everyone is going to the same place. But the people of Houston make their living in different places and ways.

Many people work in the tourism and convention industries—from promoting the city of Houston to

Houston's sprawling skyline in the early morning light.

managing large hotels. Doctors, nurses, and medical researchers work in the health care industry. Oil companies and other international businesses employ thousands of Houstonians. Researchers, scientists, and engineers work for the city's space technology and exploration center. Houston is a city of opportunity.

Thousands of tourists visit Houston each year, and tourism is a growing industry. In 1987, the George R. Brown Convention Center opened its doors. The new center made Houston second only to New York City in the amount of space it has available for convention purposes. Different conference groups have reserved space in the center through the year 2003. That means more visitors will be

spending more money, and the city will gain many new jobs.

Even many Houstonians are not aware that their city's largest employer is the Texas Medical Center. In some thirty-seven institutions such as hospitals and clinics, it provides thousands of jobs. The Texas Medical Center has plans for $1.5 billion worth of building and improvement projects. The center's directors are aiming for a higher quality and wider range of patient care and research. Already, patients from all over the world come to the city to use its excellent medical center.

Energy has been Houston's largest business since the turn of the century. Although Houston's oil companies have had to tighten their budgets,

The George R. Brown Convention Center.

Ferry boats often transport people from Houston to nearby Galveston Island.

they still remain the largest independent companies in Houston.

The city's center of international business is the Port of Houston. Nearly 200 steamship lines offer regular service to the Port of Houston from some 250 ports worldwide. During the course of a year, thousands of cargo ships from over seventy nations dock at the more than one hundred wharves of the port. Railroad and trucking lines carry in cargo to be shipped out, and haul out freight to be delivered.

The Turning Basin Terminal allows cargo to be loaded directly from ships to trucks or rail cars.

Because of the international trade, hundreds of foreign companies have set up offices in Houston. The city attracts banking branches and other companies from about sixty different countries. Big businesses are not the only companies to thrive in Houston. Thousands of independent businesses open in the city each year.

Houston, also known as Space City, is home to NASA's Johnson Space Center. People from around the world know the city as "mission control" for its spaceflight operations. The Mission Control Center controls the flight and monitors the various systems that keep the astronauts alive.

Engineers at the center research, design, and develop spacecrafts. They send the vehicles to factories to be built. Then, the engineers check flight vibrations, the vacuum of space, and how temperature changes in space and on the moon will affect the spacecraft. Visitors can take tours through the space center to learn more about how NASA functions.

Private companies have become involved with Houston's future in space, too. Among others, Grumann, Westinghouse, and Boeing have settled in Houston to research space operations.

Houston is also concerned with the future of its young people. Houston's schools work hard to provide students with a good education. Nearly a half-million students attend schools in the twenty-two school dis-

Mission Control at the Lyndon B. Johnson Space Center.

The University of Houston, University Park.

tricts in and around Harris County. Houston's Independent School District (HISD) is one of the ten largest school districts in the nation.

HISD educational leaders created "Magnet" schools which offer outstanding students programs in a wide range of fields: aerodynamics, ecology, media and communications, petrochemical careers, engineering, fine arts, health care, and special classes for gifted and high-achieving students.

Inside the Loop are two of Houston's many institutes, colleges, and universities. Rice University, located near Hermann Park, is a well-known, small private college on a beautiful, tree-covered campus. The University of Houston, Texas's second largest university, has won national attention for its research in electrical superconductors.

Other universities in the city include Houston Baptist University, Texas Southern University, and the University of Saint Thomas. Many educational health care degree programs are offered at the Texas Medical Center.

As a long day at school or work comes to an end, the setting sun reflects off the glimmering glass of the Transco Tower. Drivers again head for the freeways—another busy day in the bustling city is over.

4

Houston Proud

Although Houstonians work hard, they enjoy their leisure time, too. And, most people don't wait for the weekend to have fun. Houston residents have an exciting city to discover—parks to visit, restaurants to try, and sports events, movies, concerts, and plays to see. Houston, in fact, has been called the "year-round entertainment city."

First-time visitors to Houston are often amazed at the city's huge size and its towering buildings. Yet, the city is made up of more than just tall buildings and freeways. Pine trees and parks are spread throughout the Houston area.

Close to downtown, Hermann Park's 388 acres (155 hectares) take a full day to explore. The park's main attraction is the Houston Zoo, which has exhibits that show animals from

The Houston Livestock Parade winds down Houston's freeways.

The Children's Zoo at Hermann Park.

around the world in their natural surroundings. Special buildings house tropical birds and reptiles. The children's zoo is a small zoo in itself, where young people can pet the animals.

Outside the zoo, the Hermann Park Train chugs around a two-mile (three-kilometer) loop that curves through a dark tunnel, circles a grassy playground, and crosses a water pond. From the train, visitors can see the large overhanging canopy of the Miller Outdoor Theatre. Here, Hous-

The *Diplodocus* dinosaur attracts visitors to the Houston Museum of Natural Science.

tonians attend free concerts, plays, and festivals. People spread out on towels or lawn chairs on the grassy hill to watch the sights, or they sit under the canopy if it rains.

Also in Hermann Park is the Museum of Natural Science. In the lobby of the museum, a huge skeleton of an ancient *Diplodocus* dinosaur reaches up to the second story. The main halls lead to geographical charts of Texas, and collections of old oil well parts. Upstairs, displays of the human body explain how organs work and

computers play educational games with visitors. One of the museum's most popular exhibits is the South American Indian display of shrunken heads.

Attached to the museum is the Burke Baker Planetarium. While onlookers sit under a broad dome, gazing up into a night sky, a thirteen-foot (four-meter) projector covers the ceiling with five thousand moving stars. The computer-controlled projector also creates lifelike pictures of comets and spacecraft. The planetarium's special programs change every few months.

Near Hermann Park, the Museum of Fine Arts houses an impressive display of old and new art, including touring exhibitions. The museum also conducts a professional art school, the Glassell School, where a huge sculpture garden features works of famous artists.

Houston is well known for its arts organizations. National art critics even declared Houston the "Art Capital of the Third Coast [the Gulf of Mexico]."

The Houston Ballet Company and Houston Grand Opera both perform in the Gus S. Wortham Theater. This beautiful theater, completed in 1986, has two performance halls with a total of 3,300 seats.

At Jones Hall, the Houston Symphony has an orchestra of ninety-four musicians who perform outstanding classical concerts. During the summer, the orchestra performs under

Inside the Burke Baker Planetarium, the giant star projector creates special effects such as exploding stars and rotating planets.

Gus S. Wortham Center.

the stars at the Miller Outdoor Theatre.

The Alley Theatre is one of the country's oldest theaters. Here, plays are performed in an 800-seat main theater and 300-seat theater-in-the-round. The acting company, one of the best in the nation, brings Houston fine performances of famous plays throughout the year.

The Children's Museum in Houston is rapidly growing, and is always full of young people. Designed as an educational playground, the museum's

Children try on traditional Chinese clothing at the "Gateway to China" marketplace at the Children's Museum of Houston.

rooms offer exciting games of skill and wit. State-of-the-art computers give children a chance to test their abilities in reading and arithmetic and create their own art. In a "visual room," children dress up in different costumes to appear on an in-house television show. In the museum's miniature grocery store, attendants give kids shopping lists and send them on a spending spree.

For those interested in sports, Houston has professional teams in football, baseball, and basketball. The Summit, a large sports arena near downtown, is home to the Rockets, Houston's professional basketball team. Some of the highest paid athletes in the National Basketball Association (NBA) play on this court in

fast-paced action that thrills roaring fans. When the Rockets aren't playing, the Summit stages rock concerts, circuses, and ice shows.

The gigantic Astrodome is where the Oilers play football, and the Astros play baseball. No grass covers the stadium field—Astro-turf was invented especially for this indoor stadium.

Because of the enormous size of the Astrodome, other activities and shows use the "eighth wonder of the world" on special occasions. In February, Houston's Livestock Show and Rodeo attracts thousands of people to the Astrodome. Chuckwagon and pig races, bull riding, bronco busting, and concerts by big music stars fill the nights with fun.

On one night under the dome,

Fans cheer on their team inside the Astrodome.

teenagers line up for the "calf scramble." As loose calves run scared, the teens race through the dust and dirt, hoping to rope a calf to take home.

During this time, "Go Texan" themes spread throughout the city. Business people who usually wear suits stomp around their offices in western wear. At schools, young people learn square dancing and kick up their heels to the "Cotton-eyed Joe." The city seems to hum with country music, which keeps the Wild West spirit of Texas alive.

Some popular cartoon characters come alive at Astroworld.

Next door to the Astrodome is Astroworld, a huge amusement park. Home of the Texas Cyclone roller-coaster, Astroworld is full of rides, food stands, and shops in ten make-believe lands. Thunder River is a raft ride through "rapids."

In the same area, WaterWorld is a great place for a refreshing dip in the pool. But it's more exciting to skid down the speeding water slide, bob around in the huge wave pool, or dive from high cliffs.

When it comes to entertainment,

Houston delivers it year-round, and in many exciting ways. From a day at Astroworld to a night at the theater, Houston has something for everyone.

The people of Houston work hard to make their city an enjoyable place to live, work, and raise families.

Despite the hard times, Houstonians have worked together in the positive spirit that has long been the city's greatest strength. Houston, one of the nation's largest cities, is on the go, moving ahead, and "Houston Proud!"

Places to Visit in Houston

Astrodome
Loop 610 South and Kirby Drive
(713) 799-9544 for tours, 9555 for ticket information

Astroworld
Loop 610 South and Kirby Drive
(713) 799-1234

Battleship Texas
San Jacinto Battleground State Historic Park
La Porte
(713) 479-2411

Burke Baker Planetarium
In Houston Museum of Natural Science
Hermann Park
(713) 526-4273

Children's Museum
Allen Parkway between Shepherd and Waugh Drive
(713) 522-6873

The Galleria
5015 Westheimer at South Post Oak off Loop 610 South
(713) 622-0663

Harris County Heritage Society
1100 Bagby Street at Lamar Street
(713) 655-1912

Houston Arboretum and Nature Center
4501 Woodway at Loop 610 West
(713) 681-8433

Houston Civic Garden Center
Hermann Park
(713) 529-5371

Houston Museum of Natural Science
Hermann Park
(713) 526-4273

Houston Public Library
500 McKinney
(713) 236-1313

The Houston Sports Museum
Finger's Furniture
4001 Gulf Freeway (I-45 South at Cullen)
(713) 221-4441
A sports museum within a huge furniture store, built around the home plate of Houston's old Buff Stadium. Contains memorabilia from Houston's famous athletes.

Houston Zoo
1513 Outer Belt Drive
Hermann Park
(713) 523-5888

Jones Hall
615 Louisiana at Capital
(713) 237-1439

Museum of Fine Arts, Houston
1001 Bissonnet at Main Street
(713) 526-1361 extension 311

Museum of Medical Science
Second floor Houston Museum of Natural
Science
Hermann Park
(713) 529-3766

NASA—Lyndon B. Johnson Space Center
NASA Road Number 1 off I-45 South
(713) 483-4321

The Orange Show
2401 Munger Street near I-45 South
(713) 552-1767
A folk art tribute to the orange

Port of Houston Boat Tour
7300 Clinton Drive off Loop 610 East
(713) 225-4044 for reservations

Sam Houston Park
See Harris County Heritage Society

San Jacinto Battleground State Historic Park
3523 Highway 134, La Porte
(713) 479-2431
Includes the San Jacinto Monument

San Jacinto Museum of Texas History
San Jacinto Battleground State Historic Park
La Porte
(713) 479-2421
A museum in the base of the San Jacinto Monument

Texas Medical Center, Visitor Center
1155 Holcombe Street at Bertner Street
(713) 790-1136

WaterWorld
Loop 610 South and Kirby Drive
(713) 799-1234

Additional information can be obtained from these agencies:

Greater Houston Convention and Visitors Bureau
3300 Main Street
Houston, TX 77002
(713) 523-5050

Houston Chamber of Commerce
25th Floor, 1100 Milam Building
Houston, TX 77002
(713) 651-1313

Houston: A Historical Time Line

1836   General Sam Houston defeats the Mexican army at San Jacinto, winning independence for Texas; the Allen brothers buy land along the Buffalo Bayou and call their "town" Houston

1837   Houston becomes the capital of the Republic of Texas until 1839

1839   Houston is incorporated as a city; 10 percent of Houston's population dies from yellow fever; Austin becomes capital of the Republic of Texas

1845   Texas becomes the twenty-eighth state of the United States of America

1861   Texas withdraws from the Union and becomes a Confederate state

1865   Civil War ends and Federal troops occupy Houston; reconstruction follows

1869   The Buffalo Bayou Ship Channel Company is created and begins to develop Houston as a port

1870   A new city charter establishes eight city wards

1880   The *Houston Post* publishes its first daily newspaper

1891   The Houston Heights begins development north of the original Allen brothers' downtown Houston

1901   Oil is discovered at Spindletop and Houston starts to build oil refineries; the *Houston Chronicle* publishes its first daily newspaper

1906   Some thirty oil companies and seven banks open offices in Houston; construction begins on the city's first eight-story "skyscrapers"

1914   Houston opens its newly developed ship channel

1924   The first art museum in Texas is opened, later named the Museum of Fine Arts

1928   Houston hosts the Democratic National Convention

1946   The Texas Medical Center opens

1948   Battleship *Texas* is retired to a berth at the San Jacinto Battleground

1964   Houston becomes the center of the manned space explorations for NASA

1965   The Astrodome, the world's first indoor sports stadium, opens its doors

1969   The spacecraft *Eagle* reports to Houston that it has landed on the moon

1975   Pennzoil Place, two trapezoidal towers, opens downtown and marks a new direction in Houston's architecture

1981   Houston elects Kathy Whitmire as the city's first woman to serve as mayor

1984   Houston's oil business declines after a sharp drop in worldwide oil prices

1986   Gus S. Wortham Theater opens

1987   George R. Brown Convention Center opens

1988   Plans underway for an expanded visitors' center at NASA headquarters (designed by Disney Imagineering) and a new IMAX theater at the Museum of Natural Science

Index